My Provence

in all Zenitude...

RAFAEL. F.

My Provence

in all Zenitude...

Publisher: BoD – Books on Demand, info@bod.fr
Printing: BoD – Books on Demand, In de Tarpen 42,
Norderstedt (Germany)

Print on demand
Drawing : RAFAEL. F.
ISBN : 978-2-3221-2203-5
Legal Deposit : May 2023

PREFACE :

I was just four years old when my family and I came to live in Provence. And since then, I have never left this beautiful region; it is now almost fifty years. I have always considered myself a provençal of adoption. To be honest, if I had to leave it, it would "break my heart". I like Provençal customs and expressions so much. Not to mention the love I feel for its landscapes, its reliefs, its colors, its villages and its smells.

And then one day, I thought, "Why not discover or rediscover its authenticity with this guide?"

So I went to visit villages, cities, forests; in Luberon, Var, Alpes-de-Haute-Provence, Alpilles, etc.... Through my photos and stories, I tried to convey to you all the emotions and happiness I felt during my excursions.

I hope you will share the pleasure I had in writing *« My Provence in all Zenitude »*.

Rafael. F.

CONTENS :

CHAPTERS :

THANKS

Cassis...

When you decide to make a trip to Provence, if there is one city that remains unmissable, it is the commune of Cassis.

I have been going there regularly for many years now. And everytime, I feel this sense of discovery, the color of the water, the smells. Not to mention the sun illuminating the façades with multiple   shades that change throughout the day. It's like the photographer putting a new filter on every photo.

Area : 26,86 km²

Population : 6782 (2020)

This small Mediterranean port with narrow and intertwined streets, fraternises with a sea with such unpredictable character and its limestone cliffs where you can see a castle dating from the Carolingian Empire of the 8th century.

I love strolling by the water on these worn and time-shiny cobblestones. Looking at them, it is very easy to imagine the millions of people who have done the same thing in past centuries. Over the decades, Cassis has kept his identity. Its architecture did evolve over time, but its leaders never distorted or unravelled it.

Personally, I always make sure to arrive around noon. So I can sit on the terrace. And whether you're in winter or summer, wearing a T-shirt or a big jacket, restaurants and brasseries are always busy with tourists and locals.

I can admire these magnificent "pointus" (Marseille boats) in bright colours and so well maintained by their owners.

And if you're patient, you'll probably be lucky to see
restaurateurs buy their morning catch right on the spot.
Hard to eat fresher... right? A word of advice: listen to the
conversations that emerge from this "transaction". Because
everyone will go from his comment which will prove to be
more or less relevant, it must be admitted!

Then, in order to digest this good meal with Mediterranean
colours and flavours that will have awakened my taste buds, I walk
along the dike, on these stones with uncertain reliefs, to reach at
its end its lighthouse, polished by the whims of
the sea and the weather. And there, there is no escaping the
pleasure of the spray that will come to tread and refresh your face,
before crashing on the rocks. And if, like me, you like to meditate
or simply decompress in front of a water
reflecting the soft rays of the sun: you will be in the right
place....

But Cassis is not just a port and shaded alleys.
It is also a beautiful natural park protected and respected by its
inhabitants, where you can go hiking or cycling,
alone or with your family,
on marked and safe trails. When I go there with my
backpack and camera, I can't get enough of the scenery.

It is as if I were alone in the world in front of this beauty
that nature makes available to me. What is strange and
reassuring is the respect that walkers of all generations can have.
We speak without shouting, we greet each other by
crossing each other, we make sure to walk on the stones,
also polished by time, without ever deteriorating or tearing away
the plants. During this walk, you will also have the
opportunity, for the bravest, to swim in water of such
intense blue that it would make jealous the most beautiful
beaches called paradisiacal.

When I say "the bravest", it must be known, in all objectivity, that
the waters of Cassis are known for their invigorating
freshness. Especially if our beloved mistral visited us the
days before swimming!

However, if you do not have a sporting temperament, or the
appropriate physical ability, you will still be able to see the
Cassis Natural Park by the sea. Indeed, the city offers guided tours
of its coasts and calanques by boat, leaving from the
port. Having had the chance to do so, I can assure you that it is
worth a look.

A word of advice: in high season, remember to book a seat!

Historically, the peninsula once lived with its quarries. Their remains are still very well preserved and easily visible. It was on this site that the famous Cassis stone, renowned for its solidity and longevity, was extracted. In previous centuries, many of the kitchens in Marseille had sinks carved into this rock. Nowadays, these "batteries", as we call them in France, are sold at a high price and are often used to decorate summer kitchens. If one day you have the chance to walk on Alexandria's docks, you will tread on Cassis stone, among other places...

In short, if you are like me, if you love the beauty and authenticity of a place where you can escape for a few hours, you cannot pass Cassis without stopping!

By the way, we don't pronounce Cassis's "S." It is for the fruit that it is pronounced.

La Sainte-Baume...

The highest point is the Yoke of the Eagle and the signal of the Beguines at 1,148 metres.

Then, some forty kilometres from Cassis, stands the Sainte-Baume massif, in the commune of Plan-d'Aups-Sainte-Baume. It is with majesty that the latter comes to be
established, making the junction between the Bouches-du-Rhône and the Var.

Area : 45 000 hectares

However, it will take a few kilometres of narrow pinhead bends to reach the site. So, adorned with my backpack, a pair of walking shoes, and my inseparable camera, I am ready for my ascent.

The first feeling you get when you enter this forest is the very imposing aspect of the place. You feel so small at the feet of these trees, tens of metres high and centuries old. It is as if each of them tries to make contact with the heavens, but never succeeds. Their trunks are long and regular.

My favourite season to go there is autumn. Nature is literally changing. The colour scheme that heralds the end of summer and the beginning of winter is so beautiful and varied that it is difficult to describe it in simple words. The base of the trees and the edges of the trails are covered in a moss of a green so intense that it looks like it was painted by hand.

Even if it is only a combination of high humidity and plots that never see the sun, the result is sublime. The trunks cut by the hand of man or simply broken by the whims of nature, are also covered with mushrooms, admittedly inedible, but so pleasant to look at and immortalise. So atypical and indescribable are their forms.

With all these smells, colours and magic, you don't have to have a vivid imagination to think that at any moment you could see an elf or a fairy coming out of nowhere.

However if I can give you a little advice, stay focused on the trails. In autumn, between winding paths, centuries-old polished steps, and damp leaves that cover them surreptitiously, it is very easy to catch a gadin, as we say here. Despite this brief aside, the promenade remains largely accessible to all.

Then, when you have walked for about 45 minutes, 30 for the more experienced. That you will have come across benches carved out of the stone. That you will be refreshed at the famous Source de Nans. You will arrive as if by magic at the foot of the steps of the Dominican Sanctuary dating from the 13th century which is one with the cliff. According to legend, the first witness of Christ's resurrection lived in this Sanctuary. And one does not have to be a true believer in Christianity to feel its mysticism. The first time I crossed his threshold, I was so emotional that my eyes misted. It was as if a current of positive air had flown through me from side to side.

Up the stairs, you can admire scenes of Christ, thanks to life-size statues. In front of the church, built right in the cave, you will see a panorama of a rare beauty that will leave you breathtaking.

But I think the moment that moved me the most was when I entered the cave. The originality of this sanctuary cannot leave you insensitive. Its simplicity and uniqueness make it a special place. The humidity is so high that the drops fall continuously from the rocky vault, forming small puddles of water on its irregular soil. Allowing the candles and stained glass windows to make their reflections ripple. For those who want to pamper themselves, you will have the opportunity to sit on benches patinated by pilgrims and tourists facing an imposing altar.

Then it is full of emotion that you will come out of the monastery to finish your "pilgrimage" to the highest point of Sainte-Baume. And if you are as lucky as I am that the sky is clear, you will see Marseille and its coastline.

Generally, to conclude my trip, I always stop at the small restaurant/snack, next to the car park, to have a cold drink or a hot chocolate, depending on the season. This allows me to review my photos and thus extend this beautiful hike by thought.

Cotignac...

Then, I decided to leave the seaside, to go a little further into the
Var hinterland, to go to Cotignac; small town about forty
kilometres from Saint-Maximin. It was my first time there.
And believe me, I wasn't disappointed! A real concentrate of
discoveries of all kinds.

Having parked at the foot of the cliff, I decided to start my
journey by visiting the remains of the two towers of the
feudal castle, dating from the 11th century.

Area : 44,26 km²   *Population : 2254 (2015)*

During the ascent of the paved paths, admirably preserved
by time, I was able to admire, over the few hundred metres
to climb, quite unusual objects. Such as facade ruins that
were once certainly beautiful and large houses; or arches
dug into the rock that is now used as garages for the
inhabitants; or fountains with worn stones and covered with moss.
Not to mention the superb stone houses; or simply
this olive press so well maintained. Among the many crafts
that are very present in Cotignac, olive cultivation gives rise to
olive oil that has a high reputation beyond our Provençal borders.

I have also seen from time to time huge holes in the walls invaded by ivy. It is as if Mother Nature had wished to open a window for us to contemplate this wonderful landscape of the Var plain.

A small detail, not the least. Cotignac has several buildings listed as historic monuments. The fountain of the four seasons, the fountain of the wash house, some houses and facades, to name but a few.

And if you want an overview of these wonders created by the hand of man centuries ago, do as I do! Take the time to sit down on one of the many restaurant terraces to enjoy a good meal with regional flavours.

I couldn't leave this picturesque place without admiring its famous waterfall. But this natural spectacle is worth it. So I had to walk for about fifteen minutes through a colourful undergrowth, where the cut trunks are gradually covered with fungus, and along a small river interspersed with mini torrents, to finally reach the coveted site.

It is said to be a place of pilgrimage for couples hoping for children. But whether or not you believe in the "legend," the spectacle of this natural waterfall is breathtaking and intoxicating. Over several tens of metres, the water bleached by froth joins a steep wall where lichen, nascent vegetation and moss mix.

It is as if each plant is competing to highlight its shimmering colours.

On the way back, I thought to myself that man was capable of the worst, but he was also capable of doing magnificent things. In Cotignac, he was able to perfectly harmonise what nature had put at his disposal, with beautiful architectural creations. And above all its citizens knew how to preserve them!

Whether you like to stroll alone or with your family, if you pass by Brignoles, make a little detour by this atypical commune that will amaze your eyes and fill your curiosity.

As far as I was concerned, I was not expecting children, but expecting visual and olfactory sensations ... And Cotignac was able to meet my expectations !

Aix-en-Provence...

It is said that in Aix-en-Provence, a city founded in 123 BC, there are on average 300 days of sunshine per year. But anyway, even though I love this town, I didn't go so far as to count them. However, I still have a good excuse to go. Whether you want to go shopping, go to a restaurant or simply have a drink on the terrace.

Area : 186 km²   Population : 142 700 (2015)

I would say that Canebière is in Marseille, which the Cours Mirabeau is in Aix-en-Provence. And it is the bridge that connects the old city to the new, as a bridge would between the past and the future.

As you stroll through the alleys of Aix, also famous for its thermal baths, you will not be insensitive to the diversity of its architecture and population. Whether in summer or winter, whether it is midday or midnight, the streets are always bustling. There is a special atmosphere. Its inhabitants are serene and peaceful. They are proud to be Aix and to share their heritage with tourists from so many different countries.

I often surprise myself, sitting on the terrace, wondering where all these young people, not so young, alone or accompanied can go. Are they going to take a drama class? Visit one of the countless museums, after having joined a friend in a restaurant, surrounded by a small alley? Or simply immortalise on a canvas a setting that they can exhibit on the Cours Mirabeau or in one of the many art galleries? Let us not forget that it was thanks to Paul Cézanne, famous Aix painter (1839-1906) that our Sainte-Victoire mountain became so popular.

Aix-en-Provence has also attracted a very large student population through its cultural and ethnic diversity, its facilities and a large number of universities. Hence this special day and night life.

Aix-en-Provence has also attracted a very large student population through its cultural and ethnic diversity, its facilities and a large number of universities. Hence this special day and night life.

As I said in a previous chapter, I am not a Catholic practitioner, but I still enjoy visiting religious buildings of all faiths. And in Aix-en-Provence, if you take the time to walk the streets of the old city, you will discover a multitude of buildings of different eras and different styles. The Church of the Holy Spirit (18th century), St John of Malta (Gothic, 13th century), St Saviour (12th century cathedral), to name but a few. You will be able to immortalise magnificent statues, paintings and all kinds of church organs.

But at the bend of the alleys you will also discover fountains that have acquired a certain notoriety over the course of history. Like the Fountain of the Four Dolphins (1646), the Fountain of the Rotonde (inaugurated in 1860), the Pascal Fountain (inaugurated in 1922), or the Moussue Fountain (built in 1666) on the Cours Mirabeau which bears his name well. Since she has been able, over the centuries, to put on a real coat of foam.

There is, however, an unmissable culinary tradition in this beautiful spa, a little geometrically shaped almond paste sweetness called calisson: one of Aix's pride. Historically, its origins can be traced back to antiquity (6th century). The Persians, who love almond paste, are believed to be behind this small diamond-shaped sofa. And if you feel like it, you will have the opportunity to visit its museum, at the exit of the city, on the road to Avignon.

As you may have gathered, Aix-en-Provence is a town full of surprises and discoveries. And one day will certainly not be enough to admire everything. However, the heart of the people of Aix and its facilities are generous enough to accommodate you for several days.

Isle-sur-la-Sorgue...

How not to go to the Vaucluse without visiting L'Isle-sur-la-Sorgue (or Isles/Sorgue)? Renowned for the quality and
diversity of its antique and antique dealers, it is famous throughout the world. So much so that Japanese, British, Russian, or even wealthy Americans (to name a few) come all year round to find the rare gem they need to develop their luxurious main ... or secondary residences. Let us not forget that we are on the edge of the Luberon, famous for its
magnificent properties!

Area : 45 km²   Population : 19 480 (2015)

As an aside, if you are wondering, as I am, what is the difference between a second-hand dealer and an antique dealer, know that the first one sells its articles in the state without any guarantee; unlike the antique dealer who first carries out an expertise and provides a certificate of authenticity.

However, Isle-sur-la-Sorgue was not always the beautiful town it is today. His story proves it !

Indeed, it is said that in the Middle Ages, the first inhabitants were fishermen, living in swampy areas. Their houses were built on stilts, as floods were not uncommon. At the beginning of the 2000s, archaeological excavations even revealed the existence of a Neolithic village north of the city, dating back to 4000 BC.

But political, economic, cultural, and social upheaval in Europe did not occur until the nineteenth century. Today, the city's reputation remains unchanged because of the quality and diversity of its shops, which proudly adorn the city, as well as its activities. And believe me or not, the multiplicity of stores is often fatal to my credit card. Because I often have to use violence to resist the temptation to sell.

And if there is one activity that remains rooted in its cultural heritage, it is its Sunday market. It is one of the most beautiful in the Vaucluse. A real institution that goes back, according to the archives, to the 12th century (regulated in the 16th century). Throughout its history, this weekly event has maintained a legitimacy and a colourful spirit, thanks to the disparity of its stands installed on the docks and in its city centre.

For my part, I had the opportunity to visit this beautiful Vauclusian commune twice. The first time was in winter. Here is a little tip: if it has snowed on Mont Ventoux, that our beloved mistral is in the game, especially cover yourself well! Otherwise your day may be spoiled by the temperatures you feel....... The second time was in the summer. I have to admit that it is still more pleasant, especially for the adopted Mediterranean I am.

Usually I try to park along the Sorgue to start my day along the river. It's so soothing to hear the water slide as you walk. And if you turn even a little bit, you will notice that in some places the flow of water seems to be slowing down. It is as if the Sorgue were quieter, almost whispering in front of some buildings.

Even if in high season it is sometimes a little complicated to find a table among the many restaurants available to you, show determination! You won't be disappointed! It is a real pleasure to be able to land by the Sorgue and enjoy a meal with Mediterranean flavours and aromas. You will be able to listen to the lapping of the water between each dish. Or give a piece of bread to the green collars who are not too shy trying to lift the current, by the strength of their small webbed legs.

For those who love religious buildings, do not leave L'Isle-sur-la Sorgue without visiting the collegiate church of Notre Dame des Anges. This 17th century baroque church is a real concentration of religious ornaments. Some even compare it to a Roman church. Just that! Its two organs, the brightness of its stained glass windows, its sculptures, its gargoyles and its paintings will leave you astonished. Art lovers will even have the opportunity to visit the Villa Datris Foundation: a museum showcasing contemporary sculpture.

Personally, I am more attracted to old things.... Don't read it in pejorative terms. Indeed, I like to search for old objects. I imagine touching them what they may have seen, heard or experienced as time. Don't we say: "If this object could speak!". Some even manage to make me go back in time, remind me of a period of my life, of my childhood. Or just a person who was dear to my heart. But I have to be objective. Indeed, when your eyes carefully shift on prices, the reality check could be quite stark!

You will have understood that, regardless of the season or the number of visitors, Isles/Sorgue remains and will remain a peaceful place, full of surprises and veracity. And no need for an antique dealer to issue a "certificate of authenticity"....

Fort de Buoux...

If you are a lover of the remains of fortresses, I invite you to visit the Fort of Buoux.

In the heart of the Luberon massif (Vaucluse), you will discover the ruins of a mediaeval fort listed as a historical monument since 1986. Ideal for a family hike, or like me in solo mode with backpack and camera. Even though it is relatively easy to access, it takes about an hour to get there. A little tip: equip yourself with a good pair of walking shoes. For you will quickly notice that the stone paths are like the fort: worn out by centuries of existence and particularly slippery according to the whims of the weather.

LE FORT DE BUOUX

Les archives de Buoux ont été presque toutes détruites par le maire de la commune en1848 : « ces paperasses n'étant bonnes qu'à engendrer de la poussière »disait-il.
La forteresse de Buoux ayant joué un rôle important dans l'histoire de la ville d'Apt,l'essentiel des archives provient de cette commune.Celles ci ne débutent,pour le fort,qu'avec le XVIe siècle.Pour les périodes précédentes et les origines du fort,les seules indications viennent des fouilles et des interprétations des historiens qui ne sont pas toujours d'accord entre eux.Cela vous autorise donc à laisser libre cours à votre imagination et celle de vos enfants.

L'équipe de la mairie de Buoux vous souhaite une agréable visite et le gardien du fort se tient à votre disposition pour toute information.

ORIGINE ET HISTOIRE DU FORT

L'abbé Gay,curé de Buoux de 1.859 à 1.878 et nous dit,sans preuves :
« les romains possédaient la ville d'Apt et le fort de 123 av.Jésus Christ à 476 de notre aire.Le fort fut détruit en 731 par les Sarrasins puis reconstruit au IXe siècle par Theubert,gouverneur d'Apt ».

Pour Fernand Sauve les pointes de flèches néolithiques,les éclats de silex et les haches de pierre trouvés au cours des fouilles témoignent d'une occupation bien plus ancienne,mais comme pour le bon abbé la présence d'une occupation Romaine,selon lui, est indéniable.

En 1.975 Jean-Barruol justifiait l'occupation du fort à l'âge de bronze d'après les analyses faite par Mr. Courtin.

Aujourd'hui le chercheur Yann Codou confirme que le plateau du fort a connu une occupation importante dès l'âge de bronze et reste occupé.pendant la période gallo-romaine.

Christian Markiéwitz,l'actuel archéologue du fort date les bâtiments visibles qui sont parvenus jusqu'à nous sur une période s'étalant du XIe au XVIIe siècle .

Au XVIIe siècle le fort ayant été pris deux fois par les protestants et n'ayant plus d'intérêt militaire, Louis XIV aurait ordonné sa destruction, le fort a ensuite servi de carrière aux habitants qui s'installaient dans le vallon et sur tout le territoire de Buoux.

So it was on a beautiful October day that I decided to visit the Fort, which says it is outside the commune of Buoux. Once you have walked through the gate, which gives the impression that you are arriving at an 18th century property, you will soon be immersed in a special atmosphere. I don't know if you're like me, but when I visit old stones, I feel like I'm jumping back in time. It's like they're telling me a story. And the passage from summer to autumn often accentuates this phenomenon by delivering its colours that are both shimmering and warm. Especially when the sun has not yet had time to dry the dew and the leaves are still shining under its rays.

The days and opening hours are regulated, so you will find the guard's house at the foot of the Fort. You will be able to find out more about the rules of procedure and the history of the fortress.

As is often said, "You have nothing without nothing". Therefore, to cross the entrance to the Fort, you will have to climb a staircase dug into the cliff. Even today, the latter remains a puzzle for historians. But even if you have to be careful when climbing, try to appreciate the beauty of the scenery that will be available to you. Take a few moments to breathe this mixture of Provençal scents, such as thyme, juniper, rosemary and many others that I will let you discover.

Then after walking for about forty minutes, you will finally see the porch of the Fort of Buoux in front of you. To be honest, I was expecting something a little more impressive and grandiose. But I was soon overtaken by the majesty of the remains inside the ramparts.

Historically, the Fort was inhabited and fortified from Protohistory until the 17th century. Thus each era has made it possible to contribute to its evolution and its edification. This is why when you explore the site, you will be surprised to see the great disparity of its remains. You'll find paleochristian tombs, cave dwellings, rock silos, a mediaeval fortress, and even the ruins of a 13th-century church, to name a few. And to close it all off, the ramparts that today protect this magnificent concentrate of history.

When I see all this architectural prowess, I wonder how man ever built such buildings. Especially when you know the technical means of the time....

But if you want to appreciate the landscape even more, go up to the highest point of the Fort. And here, it will be impossible to remain in marble in front of this sublime panorama.

And if you want these moments of happiness to last, do as I do! Sit on a flat stone... and let go. Observe... Listen... Feel... what the magic of nature can put at your disposal.

Lourmarin...

Then on the way back, after about ten winding and narrow kilometres, I stopped in Lourmarin. It is said that this town is one of the most beautiful villages in France...

What struck me the most on arriving at the site was the 12th century fortress that came to impose itself on you as a knight defending his village. However, it should be noted that it was rebuilt in the 15th century by Foulques d'Agoult on the remains of the former. And it is precisely during this period that Lourmarin's population will increase sharply. This is due to the exodus of the Alpine dioceses.

Area : 20 km²　　　　　Population : 1145 (2014)

With festivals, exhibitions of all kinds and themed markets all year round, tourism is the main activity of this beautiful Luberon commune. And, in addition to its rich architectural and craft heritage, Lourmarin is known for its agriculture, its high-quality AOC wines, and a wide variety of market garden crops. Products that you can of course find in the shops of the centre, or taste in one of its many restaurants.

On the day I visited, I was lucky to find antique dealers who were exhibiting their "treasures" in the village square. And as I walked down the aisles, I could find a lava stone Buddha's head. Rarity being the price, I leave it to you to interpret my thinking.

Then, it was with pleasure that I was able to appreciate the exhibition of a Provencal painter in one of the rooms of the castle. When you look at it from an architectural point of view, you will see that the different wings were built over several centuries. This creates by redundancy a harmony of style. And I invite you to visit, among other things, this small interior courtyard where the floors and wooden landings create a column of the most atypical.

Then after taking some pictures of this technical feat, I went to admire the basin that is in the main courtyard of the fortress. It will be difficult for you to remain insensitive to the beauty of these aquatic plants, which are also diverse and varied, both in shape and colour. And if you want to deepen your knowledge of the site, you will even have the possibility to book a guided tour. Personally I have never been a fan of Indian girls, where everyone gives a speech that is "full" of relevance. Sometimes I wonder if I'm a little wild....... But that's another topic !

Then, after discovering this beautiful building, head for the city centre. The first thing that struck me was its cleanliness. Its cobbled streets, façades and fountains are so clean that you would think you were entering a movie studio. The houses are nicely planted with flowers and trees. As for shopkeepers, you can clearly feel the pleasure they take in decorating and customising their windows. Some look like real paintings straight out of a Déco magazine. The furniture in the restaurant is so chic and refined that you can enjoy it with your eyes. Nothing is left to chance.

But at the risk of shocking you, this always "nickel" aspect is not
the type of aesthetic I like the most. Personally, I prefer to visit
villages where the streets, facades, monuments are certainly
maintained, but still remain in their "juice", as they say. I like
authenticity. Perhaps I have become a little too purist with age.
But when I touch a monument, or just old stones, I like to imagine
that he or she is telling me their story.

But this is all mine! Of course! Because if Lourmarin was elected
as one of the most beautiful villages in France, it is not for nothing.

Moustiers Sainte-Marie...

When we talk about earthenware, we immediately think of
Moustiers-Ste-Marie. At the borders of the Gorges du Verdon, this
beautiful commune of the Alpes de Haute Provence is often
compared to a nursery, with its star suspended between the two
mountains. Built on the side of a cliff, it has remained the capital
of earthenware since the 17th century.

Area : 88 km²   Population : 686 (2014)

There are villages that you never tyre of seeing and seeing again. It is as if each visit brings its own new set of discoveries. And this is one of them! However, in order to appreciate even more the panorama that will be offered to you, I invite you to park in the lower part of the village. You will have the privilege of admiring these houses built from the restaurants; sublimated by the olive trees that, thanks to their shades of green, illuminate the façades that have aged for centuries.

Historically, the monastery of Beauvoir was founded by monks from the island of Lérins (Alpes Maritimes) in 433. The latter was built on the heights of Moustiers. His ancestry, both geographically and morally (of course, I'm talking about the days when the church played a very important role in the lives of villagers), is akin to a shepherd tending to his flock.

Although I don't think the building is particularly interesting, I would still advise you to take the time to go there. You will be able to discover a style ranging from the Renaissance, to Gothic through a Romanesque nave. However, appropriate footwear is strongly recommended.

Even though the 15-minute climb is easy, the paved path is particularly slippery in all seasons. That's probably why, our forebears had been installing bodyguards all the way up.

But, while the ascent did not come in a spectacular way, it was the panorama that struck me the most. And if, like me, the sky is favourable to you, it is a 180° view that will delight your curiosity. This view of the lake, this valley as far as the eye can see and this green vegetation are simply magical.

And when I look closer, I think that today it is rare to be able to admire such a landscape, without modern infrastructure that alters the natural beauty of the site. It remains to be seen until when !

However, even though the monastery is of historical interest in relation to the origin of the commune, it is nevertheless faience that has made it known. And this thanks to the fineness of its clay, the quality of its water and its wood. In 1929, Moustiers opened its faience museum, where the most beautiful pieces from the 17th century to today are exhibited in no less than five rooms.

I don't know about you, but personally when I visit a village, I enjoy sitting in a small restaurant to honour regional cuisine. So I can observe the people, admire the landscape and the facades. I imagine all these wonders taking the time to tell me their story.

And in Moustiers, there is no shortage of restaurants. It's like the pottery shops that showcase their local crafts, offering souvenirs that can be bought on any budget. Who hasn't seen a Moustiers in someone's house at least once in their life? It's important to know that these crafts are exported around the world. Even more so today with the advent of the Internet !

Then take the time to stroll through the streets of this beautiful Provencal commune. Here you can admire its cobbled streets, fountains, waterfalls, small church and displays of all kinds of souvenirs.

Because even if Moustiers faience is often imitated......it is rarely equalled ! And, as I often say, "nothing beats authenticity"!

Forêt de Saint-Pons...

If you are like me and you particularly enjoy walking in the forest,
I highly recommend the one in St-Pons. Comfortably located in the
commune of Gémenos, it is particularly appreciated by hiking
enthusiasts. The reason I'm insisting on this is that bikes are
banned on the site, as are our four-legged friends, moreover.
Which I find somewhat paradoxical, because dogs can sometimes
be cleaner than some disrespectful people...... But anyway!

Area : 752 hectares dont 52 aménagés

This natural park, created by the Marquis d'Albertas at the end of the 18th century in the Gemenos seigneury, has the particularity of being located in a valley protected from the winds. And it is thanks to its stream (from the source of St-Pons) and its microclimate that over the centuries it has acquired a lush vegetation.

In the past, it was St. Martin's Chapel that was home to the parishioners of Gemenos. But even if today it remains closed, you will still have the opportunity to admire its exterior at the entrance of the estate.

I remember that the first time I went to the site, I was like the mill of St-Pons. I thought, "How did man and nature come together and do this?" The waterfall takes this rock in its arms, which is itself draped in a foam that has grown over the years. Not to mention these small locks made of metal stung by rust and aged by time, limiting the flow of water so that hikers can enjoy their uniqueness for longer.

However, the unmissable building on the grounds of St. Pons turns out to be its monastery. The latter, having been elevated to the rank of abbey in 1223, thanks to a religious community of women, was abandoned in 1407. The abbey now belongs to the regional council which has generously contributed to its complete restoration. And even if today it is a little complicated to visit it, take the time to sit in the meadow, to admire the beauty of its structure, the finesse of its sculptures, its woodwork and its gargoyles that have been watching over it for so long.

And generally, it is still under the charm of these architectural exhibitions that I begin the ascent of a perfectly marked forest domain.

What is particularly noticeable about this forest is the fact that you can adapt your path according to your age and physical condition. And the icing on the cake is that it is not unusual to come across a horse and a rider on the way.

Another advantage of St-Pons is that you can walk there all year round. Its paths allow you to walk in the shade as well as in the sun, depending on the time and the season. This is all the more reason to discover these intertwined paths that will inevitably lead you to an atypical place. Like a high point that will offer you a 360° view, or La Glacière, or much more accessible: its beautiful waterfall of the Gour de l'Oule.

But a common place with all these points of interest is the diversity and quality of its flora. Throughout your walk, you will feel immersed in typical Provençal vegetation and protected by majestic trees that man has respected.

And even if sometimes the somewhat high "volume" of some hikers disturbs the singing of birds, or the serenity of a small animal, soak up this "front" made graciously available to you. Rejuvenate, let go and enjoy the moment!

Avignon...

Avignon is what we call a must-see of the Vauclusian region. It is difficult not to fall under the spell of its mediaeval ramparts, its gothic-style palace and its famous bridge that gave birth to a continent that everyone has sung at least once in their life...

Historically, in the fourteenth century, Avignon was the seat of the papacy, in direct competition with the Vatican. And if today we still call it the City of the Popes, it is because they lived there from 1309 to 1423.

Area 65 km²   Population : 92130

I usually park outside the ramparts to admire its bridge, which used to connect the two sides of the Rhône. I imagine the villagers walking past with their waggons full of goods, pulled by weakened horses to sell or barter their meagre spoils, in the surrounding countryside. But even though today only half of the building remains, it is still open to the public for a few euros. Thus giving the most curious, the possibility to contemplate a remarkable panorama as well as this stone breastplate that has protected, for centuries, the palace and its inhabitants.

Then, after daydreaming for a few minutes, I zigzag through the narrow cobbled streets of the fortification to the Place de l'Horloge. I love this place... There is a special atmosphere. Perhaps it is due to the imposing architecture of his town hall and its colourful carousel opposite; or to the imposing stature of his opera house.... I don't know!

But to appreciate the singularity of the place even more, sit on one of the many terraces. Once you have settled down, take a moment to observe the decoration of the restaurants. You'll notice that they all have artist posters, performance posters. After all, the Popes' Palace is not the city's main attraction.

Of course, I want to talk about its famous festival, which takes place every year. Many famous and aspiring artists have performed there. A little tip: if you want to book a hotel room during this period, book early. After all, they are often overrun by aficionados and tourists. And I would be speaking ill when I say it's no coincidence that fares go up during the festivities.

For the record, it was founded in 1947 by Jean Vilar. But it was not until 1963 that its founder agreed to share its patronage and artistic orientation.

However, the main 'attraction' of Avignon remains the City of the Popes, built in less than twenty years (1335-1352) thanks to Benedict XII for the Pontifical Palace (called old palace) and Clement VI for its extensions (new palace). Even if in the past Avignon was already an important city, the construction of the Palace has contributed greatly to its demographic and economic expansion.

If you want to "explore" the labyrinth of the building, there are three possibilities. Either on a classic tour, or with a guide who will explain the subtleties of this jewel; or with a digital tablet that will be handed to you at the reception. Whatever option you choose, I am sure you will be amazed by the delicacy of the architecture and the grandeur of the place.

But if one takes a closer look at the enormous scale of the sites that were once being built, one realises how powerful the Church was; both financially and politically. Not to mention the power it held over the people.

Today, even if its superiority is null and void in the so-called "modern" countries, we still have its architectural heritage which is not about to die off. I do not think that the same can be said of contemporary constructions.

La Barben...

In the region, when you think of the town of La Barben, you immediately think of its animal park.

But you should know that this famous zoo located in the middle of the Bouches-du-Rhône, must share its notoriety and its hectares with its castle. Or should I say its fortress of the 11th century, inhabited by King René in the 15th century. If you take the time to visit it, you can admire its magnificent French garden designed by Le Nôtre, creator notably of the gardens of the Palace of Versailles...... Depending on the time of year, you may even be able to visit the interior, with its rooms still furnished, and see how admirably conserved and maintained this building has been for so many centuries.

Area : 2000 hectares   Population : 823

To be completely transparent with you, I'm trying to offer in this tour guide a variety of tours. Old villages, forest walks, remains of fortresses, or family outings in an animal park such as this one, which is also open all year round. A little over a decade ago, I visited the Barben Zoo with my family. When I decided to go back, I did so with some reluctance.

Let me explain. I love animals of all kinds. As a result, I find it very difficult to see them locked up in more or less confined spaces. But, as they say: "Only fools don't change their minds!"

First, let's go back to the origins of the region's largest animal park. It was founded in 1971 by a passionate agricultural engineer named André Pons.

It was only 17 years later that, for personal reasons, he ceded the management of the site to the SARL Parc Zoologique. Its buyers' primary objective was to promote species conservation and educate visitors with explanatory panels.

Today, the zoo has about 700 animals with more than 120 different species, terrestrial and aquatic. A small detail that is not the least, their well-being depends only on the price of starters, bars/snacks spread over the park and its pretty souvenir shop. One employee said that the animal park did not receive any subsidies. So, even if you find some rates a little excessive, tell yourself that you are doing a good deed!

When I walked through the park gate to start the tour, one thing immediately struck me as I watched the animals. You immediately feel that they are very well cared for. They're serene. Cats show no aggressiveness behind their windows. Primates play under the tender eyes of visitors. Hippopotamuses sleep quietly in their s paces. Rhinoceroses share their meal quietly. The same applies to all species. So you can take the time to look at them and photograph them in peace.

But I think there's a causal relationship in all of this positivity.
Indeed, you will find that animals live in spacious spaces, with
infrastructure made of quality and eco-responsible materials.
Because management makes it a point to be environmentally
friendly.

For the lunch break, you can choose to picnic under a tree or in the
sun on one of the many facilities available. And if you prefer a meal
tray, opt for one of the snack bars. It is true that the budget will
not be the same and there will be nothing in it, but once again "it is
for the right cause".

In short, as you will have understood, I took great pleasure in
repeating my visit to the zoo of La Barben. And whether you are
small or large, with your family, as a couple or even alone, it will be
difficult not to fall under the spell of all these marvels with hair,
feathers or scales.

I would like to reward all those who care for, manage and maintain
animals and this magnificent animal park. Because on a daily
basis, it can't be simple! A drop in attendance, complicated
weather conditions... or a pandemic, can very quickly call
everything into question....

Ansouis...

When I arrived in Ansouis, the first idea that came to mind was that of Mother Nature laying this "Provençal nativity scene" on a huge rock at the foot of the Luberon.

But you should know that this beautiful town was originally not intended for tourist purposes, quite the contrary... Its history begins in the Xth century. The military fortress was built to protect the Aigues valley from invaders. At the time, only a few buildings kept him company.

Area : 18 km²   Population : 1051 (2015)

It was not until the 16th century and the end of the religious wars that the building was transformed into a dwelling. Then another century the Escalis family built outbuildings with gardens.

He came to symbolise the aristocratic way of life in the Enlightenment. A small recommendation: if you wish to visit the interior of the castle and its gardens, enquire beforehand about the opening days and hours.

When I discover or rediscover a village, there is always something that catches my eye. As for Ansouis, what struck me the most were the facades. They are extraordinarily unique. All period dwellings have frames carved and fashioned from thick blocks of stone. And centuries, mixed with the elements, have only refined their delicacy and accentuated their authenticity. It is not for nothing that this municipality has been classified as one of the "most beautiful villages in France" since June 1999.

Today, this pretty little village has been able to develop its tourism and agriculture thanks to its wineries and olive groves. Local products that you will, of course, have the pleasure of finding in the shops of Ansouis. Not to mention its guest houses that will welcome you with simplicity and professionalism, in beautiful houses.

I don't know about you, but personally I'm more gourmet than greedy. Therefore, when I visit a village, I cannot resist a table with Provençal colours and flavours. I like to pay tribute to all the love a chef can put into his culinary creations. If I were to advise you of an establishment, it would be "Le Grain de Sel". I discovered a place full of sincerity, both in human and in taste, with a very reasonable addition. The latter also includes the privilege of being able to have lunch facing a panorama that many would envy us.

If you need to spend one or more nights in Ansouis, you should know that apart from the discovery of this magnificent region, Ansouis has many activities to offer you. Among the "must-see" sites are the Museum of Wine Arts and Crafts, the Extraordinary Museum, St. Martin's Church dating back approximately to the 12th century (there is a lack of writings on its history). For the more romantic ones, its balcony that will open the horizon to the Luberon valley. And for lovers of miniatures, I invite you to discover the workshop of the santonnier, voted best worker of France in 2004.

As you will have understood, the size of a municipality is not proportional to the pleasures and discoveries it can generate.

Barjols...

Very often, I had the opportunity to cross the commune of Barjols, without ever taking the time to stop there. Barjols, meaning "pretty hills" in Provençal, is a real concentrate of relics, culture and sites that have, over the centuries, made it possible to build its history.

Its origins begin in the 12th century. Thanks to the omnipresence of water, due to the many springs that pass through it, Barjols will quickly develop its activities and its economy around this precious element. But it is his tanneries that will make his reputation. The first was born in 1601 thanks to Jean-Baptiste Vaillant and the tax advantages granted by Henri IV. In 1782, there were 24 such unions. In the early twentieth century, workers treated mainly hides and skins from Africa, Asia, and South America.

Area : 30 km²   Population : 3051 (2015)

The tanneries of Barjols reached their peak in the 1950s. But the discovery of chromium tanning and the increasing competition will cause their decline. A succession of bankruptcy filings followed, followed by the final closure of the last plant in 1983. However, when you walk around the city, you can still visit the old premises rehabilitated into workshops and galleries of all kinds.

Another particularity has made the reputation of this village: its 24 fountains and washrooms. And the fact that they were built over several eras made them special. Not only are these buildings all more beautiful than each other, but they have also made life easier for villagers.

Generally, I try to recommend you a nice table to eat. But this time I will abstain.... Because that day I have to admit that I was not very lucky...

This small negative point did not in any way alter my desire to know more about this beautiful commune, I then went to the famous waterfall and its convent of Carmes which overlooks it.

Whether you are a Barjolese or a tourist, it is difficult not to succumb to the charm of this little corner of paradise. This colourful waterfall, several tens of metres high with the rays of the sun that caress it before jumping into this water reservoir in a "bancau" (difference in height in Provence), is just sublime. According to reports, this place of relaxation would be very appreciated by walkers who are looking for a water point to cool down, but also by lovers... The inscriptions carved on the tree trunks and stones for several decades attest to this!

Then, once you have taken the time to admire or "back down" in front of this magical place offered by Mother Nature, I invite you to join the Convent of the Carmes. However, I must warn you that the stairs leading to it are rather steep, but nevertheless very well laid out.

Historically, the "Carmes brothers", made up of lay people, pilgrims and crusaders, tired of religious wars, were born in the 12th century. They created the convent in cave dwellings in 1670, but later industrialised a century later. Inside, you can still see pipes dating from that era, mingling with the "stigmas" of his hotel, and then visit the underground galleries. All these remains are open to the public during the day.

In short, Barjols is a commune in the Var hinterland that has managed to develop discreetly. It has succeeded in providing a historical, geological and cultural heritage that has delighted and will delight many generations in its centuries of existence.

Roussillon...

Among all the villages of the Lubéron, there is one that remains unmissable: Roussillon. Located at the foot of the Vaucluse mountains and in the heart of the world's largest ocher deposit, this town owes its reputation to its cliffs and open-air ochre quarries.

Area : 30 km²   Population : 1328

When I arrived in Roussillon, the first image that came to mind was that of a painter laying down his canvas, playing with shades of red, yellow, pink and purple delicately shaping each outline of these typically Provençal houses.

This is one of the reasons why many artists such as Jean Cocteau, Carzou, Buffet or Ambrogiani have put down their personal belongings to enjoy the atypism that characterises this place. But it's not just the site's uniqueness that has made its reputation. As I said earlier, Roussillon owes its reputation to the quality of its ochres. Indeed, its pigments have been used, for generations, by painters and masons to dye facades. The quarries, operated since the 17th century, employed up to a thousand people until the late 1930s.

Nowadays, they can be visited on perfectly laid out and regulated paths, in order not to degrade anything. It should be noted that it is strictly forbidden to collect this precious 'Holy Grail', or face a fine. As you wander through this brightly coloured entity, it's very easy to see why the place needs to be protected. Ochre deposits are as beautiful as they are ephemeral. That is why we must enjoy its beauty and respect this fairy rock, so that future generations can also discover "The Way of the Ochres".

Then at lunch time, it was with all their professionalism and happiness that the owners of the restaurant "La Treille" welcomed me. What could be more pleasant than to eat under an arbour shared between sun and shade, surrounded by façades with authentic colours and architecture. And when the quality of the place precedes a meal cooked with fresh products, with Provençal flavours, what more could you ask for? I don't know about you, but when I sit down, I like to listen to linguistic diversity. Try to recognise where some tourists may come from! Even a little chat with them. I find that kind of exchange very rewarding. Which is a bit paradoxical, I admit, with my rather lonely character!

The church of Roussillon was built from carved stone, at the top of the village and inside the ramparts to ensure its protection, between the 11th and 12th centuries. The facade as we know it today dates back to the 17th century. We owe it to the sculptor Alexis Poitevin of Roussillon.

The day you go to this beautiful village of Luberon, do as I do, take the time to admire the narrow streets, the façades coloured by this ochre renowned throughout the world. Take these old staircases, worn out by the whims of time, to make the streets communicate in "bancau", as a breadcrumb would do.

Stop in front of these ramparts that would have so much to tell us if they could talk. All those periods of war, lull, destruction and reconstruction they have known and survived.

Then to conclude this beautiful journey, do as I do, sit on a bench and soak up this beautiful valley of the Luberon.

I often wonder about the fact that we tend to go thousands of miles away to get what we can find not far from home. Without being jingoistic, I think to myself that I am really lucky to live in such a beautiful region...

Fontaine-de-Vaucluse...

For many decades, the Fontaine-de-Vaucluse has remained a real mystery for geologists. Dives were not organised until the 20th century.

Area : 7,1 km²   Population : 643 (2015)

Thanks to these various shipments, many valuable coins were reassembled. For in ancient times, the Fountain was a place of ritual offerings. These explorations also revealed that the source was the only exit point from an underground basin 1100 km long, bringing together various nearby geological sites.

But history is not just about coins. Over the centuries, the Fontaine -de-Vaucluse has been able to maintain legends of dragons and nymphs, revealing a little more mystery in this already very singular place. And develop by redundancy a mercantile opportunity for souvenir shops...

From a practical point of view, allow me to offer you a little piece of advice! If you decide to go there in high season and on Sundays, adopt the "zen attitude" ... To park, go directly to the large car park provided for this purpose at the entrance of the commune.

These minor inconveniences are the counterpart of this notoriety that the site has been able to exploit, in a positive way, since the 1980s. Indeed, you will quickly realise that the residents offer their visitors many activities. For example, you can visit "The Jean Garcin History Museum 39-45".

You will discover for the youngest, or rediscover for the elders, how complicated this period of our history was, thanks to the most realistic reconstructions.

For those who love caving, you can walk through the maze of galleries in the "Underground World Museum".

Then, as you go out, you will stroll along the stands to admire the finesse of the art of crystal, Provencal crafts and why not buy some souvenirs.

What is pleasant about this Vauclusian city is the possibility of having lunch by the water almost everywhere. And this is thanks to a large number of restaurants accessible to all budgets. But for lovers of picnics with family or lovers, I am sure you will find a nice place fitted out for this purpose. As far as we are concerned, we have set our sights on "La Pointe Noire".

A restaurant taken over and restored a few months ago by a team combining a perfect mix of professionalism and sympathy. As for the quality of their dishes, it is the image of their "showcase". All served on a pleasant terrace with the sound of the river in the background.

It was in the early afternoon that we climbed to what turned out to be the main attraction of this tourist spot. To be honest, I'm not sure we picked the best time. It is to be expected that after the meal the visitors want to give themselves a good conscience by burning their calories at lunch!

What struck me most, when we arrived at the Fountain, was the clarity of this almost turquoise water where this white cliff, several tens of metres high, is reflected. You feel so small and vulnerable in front of such a geological wonder. You should know, however, that its level and flow rate vary according to the seasons... They are inversely proportional to its attendance rate. In high season, many tourists for a rather low fountain, and vice versa!

In short, if I were to summarise this place in a few words, I would say that this municipality offers a concentration of activities on a geographical area equally concentrated. But you will have understood, depending on your expectations, choose your period to go there. Because the Fontaine-de-Vaucluse will charm you and welcome you in all seasons!

La Sainte-Victoire...

In all humility, I can say that it is a privilege to live at the foot of Sainte-Victoire ... If today it is famous throughout the world, it is thanks to the painter Paul Cézanne who has immortalised it nearly 80 times. Every day I can see the colour palettes it gives us, varying with the weather and the seasons.

So with every new hike, it's like I'm discovering it for the first time. For even if I know the main paths, I will not have enough of a life to learn all the mysteries and nooks of its paths.

Aria : 160 km²   Altitude : 1011 mètres

Mount Venturi, in the Provence region, is a young mountain that, according to satellite surveys, taken between 1993 and 2003, is still growing by 7 millimetres per year. But this is not the only particularity. Indeed, due to its geographical location, it has a wide range of Mediterranean vegetation on its southern slope and alpine on its northern slope, with 900 listed floral species. This would represent 20% of the French flora. As far as fauna is concerned, 27 species of mammals and 126 species of birds have been recorded to date.

It is therefore thanks to its typically Mediterranean climate and its well-marked paths, depending on their difficulties, that you will be able to appreciate the Sainte-Victoire mountain. What makes it so popular with locals and tourists alike is the fact that it can accommodate a diverse audience. Whether you are a family, a couple or alone; whether you are a fan of mountain biking, hiking or climbing; everyone will find something to enjoy! But there is a high price to be paid for all of this: RESPECT.

By that I mean that we should not do anything at a place that offers us such uniqueness. For example, walking or riding (for bicycles) on the paths provided for this purpose, letting nature grow so that your neighbour can admire it, and above all not throwing your waste anywhere! I'm not even talking about cigarette butts!

For in the twentieth century, it experienced three great fires. The first was provoked by the German army in 1944 to flush out a group of resistance fighters. The second was on August 25, 1986. A young volunteer firefighter will unfortunately die there. Then, three years later, between the Bimont and Pourrières dams, five thousand hectares will be ravaged by flames, following clearing work.

But Sainte-Victoire is not just a hiking trail. She also has her story. Indeed, during your trip, you will have the opportunity to see Celto-Ligure remains, attesting to a very ancient presence on the site. A chapel built in the 13th century on one of the mountain peaks. You can also cross and admire the two dams. First, the Zola dam built between 1850 and 1854, then the Bimont dam built between 1946 and 1951. For the bravest, do not hesitate to "swallow" a few more kilometres to join this 19 metre high cross located at the top of the Eperon, inaugurated in 1875.

Then, to perfect your knowledge of this place that I think is one of the ineluctable places of the Aix country, stop at "La Maison Sainte-Victoire", located in the commune of Saint-Antonin. In addition to a small educational museum, she will tell you that her land has been farmed for many decades. Every year, olive oil and wine with typical Mediterranean flavours and flavours are produced. Local products that the chef of the restaurant with the same name will sublimate on your plates. All of this is served by a team that provides an impeccable welcome.

Purists would tell you that without this beautiful Provence sun, these regional products would never be what they are! Not only does its land delight our taste buds, but the 'Cézanne mountain', as some call it, offers a pink marble that has made it possible to build large houses nearby.

As you will have understood, even if this beautiful mountain has not yet finished growing, we must remain sensitive to the fact that it is fragile and that we must know how to preserve it at all times. All this goes through gestures that must become automatic during your walks. In Buddhism, people speak of the "impermanence" of what surrounds us. But just because nothing is eternal does not mean that we should hasten its decline. So let's think of future generations who will walk in our footsteps and discover the fauna, flora and geology of this beautiful Sainte-Victoire!

Les Baux-de-Provence...

It is difficult not to fall under the charm of this commune in the heart of the Alpilles mountains. When you enter this fortress built between the 11th and 13th centuries, it is as if you were going back in time. You would almost expect to come across characters in period clothing at the bend of a street. This is probably one of the reasons why many filmmakers regularly pose their cameras there. What could be more beautiful than natural scenery?

Area : 18 km²   Population : 361

But this "fortified belt" perched on its 7-hectare rock, with its entirely cobbled streets, is still more a tourist destination than a real place to live. Only 22 out of 361 inhabitants live inside the ramparts.

Originally, the building was designed to control and protect 79 surrounding towns and villages. Economically, it was not until 1822 that the geologist Pierre Berthier discovered bauxite, which would be mined until the end of the twentieth century.

But even if today it no longer plays a patriarchal role on the valley, that its deposit is exhausted, it nevertheless wants to preserve its architectural and cultural heritage. This is done in order to host throughout the year festivals such as the Carrière des Lumières, the Salon des Santons (with its 17th century collection), the Festival of Photography, exhibitions of paintings and sculptures... In 2018, nearly a million and a half people visited the site. In the past, many painters such as Van Gogh, Seyssaud and Picasso, who recognised the original essence of the Baux-de-Provence, stayed there for longer or shorter stays.

When you visit this cinema-like site, take time to appreciate its 22 historic monuments. Even if the centuries have overcome some, they have kept all their authenticity and charm. It's like an old lady who hasn't lost the beauty of her youth. As I have said many times, I would like to see these old stones tell me what they have seen or heard during all these centuries of existence. They would have so much to tell us...

When I walk around an unusual place like this, I always try to find a restaurant that is just as special. That day, behind a tall iron gate, I saw a small interior courtyard with impeccable taste. This nugget is nicely called "Les Baux Jus". Everything is done to make the customer feel as if they were "caught up" in a cloud of zeal. As for the welcome, the interior and the products offered a la carte, they are in perfect harmony with this serenity that is emerging.

Then after that pure moment of tranquillity, I wandered through the alleys. So I was able to discover, or rediscover for some, small craftsmen who make objects in front of your eyes that it is difficult to resist, so much their creators put all their knowledge and their heart to give them life.

When you visit the St Blaise Chapel of the 12th century and Saint Vincent Church of the 16th century, you realise how much religion there used to be. For despite their sobriety, two religious buildings on such a small territory, it gives us food for thought!

Les Baux-de-Provence is not just a collection of craft shops and restaurants. As an aside, I highly recommend that you book a table in advance, especially in high season! It is also the remains of a magnificent castle and a museum dedicated to it. For a few euros, you will walk in the footsteps of soldiers who used to protect the valley from invaders. Throughout the journey, explanatory panels will answer your questions. Reconstructions of weapons of war, such as catapults, will plunge you into the feudal world. You will also tread stairs with cramped steps, which centuries have polished and made slippery. And there, several dozen metres away, the "Holy Grail": a 360° view over the whole valley.

So if you want to go back in time and discover a tourist site known for its authenticity for generations, do not hesitate to visit, alone or with your family, the Baux-de-Provence. Its ramparts will immerse you in its history rich in events, with its relics and buildings that "the keepers of time" have preserved so well during all these centuries.

Oppède-le-Vieux...

It is now several months since I started this beautiful adventure.
And I keep discovering new villages in this part of Provence called
Luberon. It is for me a real resurgence of places all more singular
than each other. However, they do have one thing in common,
namely the time scars inscribed on the stones of their façades.
They are like abstract encyclopaedias, eager to tell stories.

Area : 24 km²   Population : 1389 (2015)

Located on the northern side, Oppède-le-Vieux is recommended not only for lovers of old stones, but also for lovers of hikes of all kinds. Its 16th century castle and collegiate church will take you back to the Middle Ages.

It was not until the beginning of the 20th century that the villagers descended into the valley to create the hamlet of Oppède-les-Poulivets. Not only was land more accessible, but it also proved more fertile. The inhabitants gradually relocated the town hall (1912), the post office, the communal school, and created some businesses. Consuelo Saint-Exupéry, the wife of the famous writer, even took refuge there in 1940. She stayed there for two years before joining her husband in the United States. She will even dedicate a book on her Provencal stay at the end of the decade.

Nevertheless, the main attraction of the site remains its 13th century fortress. Built on the heights of the village, it has continued to watch over the Oppedis for hundreds of years.

The advanced decay of this architectural feat is not only due to the vagaries of time. Abandoned in the 17th century, the castle experienced a terrible earthquake in 1731.

It was never rebuilt, but it served as a stone quarry until the early 19th century. Today, this "shellfish limestone" is very appreciated by chimney manufacturers for its many qualities. The stone of Oppède will contribute to the building of the Palais des Papes in Avignon and the dome of the White House.

I must admit that when I arrived on the site, all my senses were solicited. I felt that in these places, nature was still the master of it own destiny. It was as if man did not want to upset the natural alliance between this lush vegetation and the façades that had crossed the centuries.

At first, I stayed in the heart of the village square, like a statue in the pit of an amphitheatre that would contemplate these buildings built on the mountainside.

At first, I stayed in the heart of the village square, like a statue in the pit of an amphitheatre that would contemplate these buildings built on the mountainside.

But before I walked through the narrow streets to discover houses built on the cliffs, in complete harmony with the terrain, I took the time to eat. I didn't have to look very far! Just behind me was a charming little restaurant with a vintage style... Everything I love! "Nostalgia when you hold us!" And the school's bosses greeted me with kindness and professionalism. I was able to taste an assortment of dishes, with flavours and regional scents that did not have to go many miles to come to embellish this colourful "discovery tray".

If you take the time to walk in the old village, you will discover how well it has kept all its authenticity and charisma. I know that this term is generally used for an individual, but in this case, I will take the liberty of making an exception. However, I strongly advise against town shoes. The uneven paving stones can be quite disconcerting. A "gadin" arrived so quickly!

So if your destiny intersects with that of this beautiful little commune, come and discover and understand why I fell under the charm of this place so atypical. A haven of serenity where time seems to have stopped, where nature is not stressed by modern life. In short, a small village where it is good to live in peace....

Sanary-sur-Mer...

Unlike some places we discovered together, Saint-Nazaire, which became Sanary in 1898, is a well-known commune on the Var coast.

What is less important, however, is a very specific period in its history which, in my view, has changed its fate. This is certainly why these 'pure' inhabitants, with whom I had the opportunity to converse, did not take long to convince me of how attached they were to their city, and even a little 'chauvinistic' for some.

Area : 19 km²   Population : 17 000

First of all, it should be noted that this small Var port has only been recognised as a tourist hotspot for about forty years. As you stroll through these intertwined alleys, as you gaze out at the stylish and unusual windows, it is hard to imagine what happened during World War II.

Indeed, during this complicated period, and in order to escape the rise of Nazism, Sanary was for many German and Austrian intellectuals a "land of exile." At the time, if the Sanaryans had not shown compassion and humanism, many people would have seen their destiny turned upside down. As a result, as many as 500 refugees tracked by the enemy were able to hide there. In 39-45, it was even nicknamed "Sanary-the-Germans". You will recognise that "Sanary-sur-Mer" makes you dream a lot more!

In 1942, it was invaded by the German army. To clear a firing line, the invader destroyed many classified buildings. The allies, for their part, will only make matters worse by retaliating. As a result of this heavy damage, the city received on November 11, 1948, the "War Cross 39-45".

In order to hide from the Nazis, the famous oceanographic explorer Jacques-Yves Cousteau (to name but a few) had to move to Sanary. And it is in the villa "Le Baobab" that he will hide his breathing apparatus in deep water, so that it does not fall into the hands of the enemy. Subsequently, many works related to scuba diving will be carried out and then tested in Sanaryan waters. The Frédéric DUMAS museum will even be dedicated to underwater archaeology.

But it will take many years before the stigma of war fades to make way for a better place to live.

Over the last few decades, the "city keepers" have managed to exploit the tourist network, offering numerous activities on land and sea. For example, you can take a boat trip and admire the beauty of the coast and its seabed.

On the dock, the smell of freshly caught fish, placed on an ice bed, will tickle your senses. And if you prefer to taste the treasures of the sea, without having to cook them, trust the talent of the chefs who will delight your taste buds! Then, at the bend of a narrow alley, you can also visit one of the many churches and chapels, built between the 15th and 19th centuries. Fortunately, the city was able to protect them from the painful events of the past!

But this place is above all a place of tranquillity, where it is good to live, where the inhabitants have kept this "village" spirit. Far from the often overrated places found in some neighbouring towns. This is probably the reason why, in 2018, its daily market was elected "most beautiful French market". Not forgetting the night craft market, from June to September, so popular with tourists and locals.

All this to say that if you like the authenticity of a small Mediterranean port, if you want to eat a regional dish by the water or in a charming little crossroad, stop at Sanary-sur-Mer! Do as many painters, writers, filmmakers, inventors who have, thanks to this little "cocoon", managed to find inspiration.

Pernes-les-Fontaines...

Pernes-les-Fontaines: what a nice name to call this Provencal village located in the heart of the Luberon!
But it was not until 1936 that he was so named. Its 12th century fortress, meanwhile, began to see fountains built in the second half of the 18th century. Nowadays, the main attraction of the town, no less than forty of them share the mediaeval city.

Area : 51 km²   Population : 9566

As I strolled through the alleys, I felt that each had a mission to look out for its inhabitants. I even went so far as to imagine that over the centuries, each fountain would have become a bit like their confidante. Residents come to tell him unspeakable secrets hidden from prying eyes, fearing that they will be surprised by gossip mongers. Thus becoming, from generation to generation, the living memory of this beautiful fortified enclosure.

Having been built over such a long period of time has helped to create a certain architectural singularity. Nevertheless, among all these creations, it is the fountains "Gigot" (near the Ferrante Tower) and "Cormoran" (facing the Covered Hall), which over the centuries have been able to distinguish themselves from their "little sisters".

But if you wish to admire as many fountains as possible, I invite you to withdraw a detailed and commented plan from the Tourist Office. Thus, you can, in a playful way, discover this forty monuments, while appreciating the particularity of the façades, frescoes and floral decorations. But Pernes is also a place where you can stay in a hotel or guest room with unrivalled charm, take time to visit the Comtadin Costume Museum, the 11th-century Church of Our Lady of Nazareth, the 17th-century Covered Hall, or the 11th-century Clock Tower.

However, before it became a tourist site, Pernes-les-Fontaines made a significant contribution to the history of Luberon, and by redundancy to that of our beautiful Provence. Indeed, as I said earlier, the fortress was built in the 12th century. Dominated by a dungeon overlooking the entire city, it was built by the family of the counts of Toulouse who, although they did not live in the commune, ruled it with an iron fist.

It will take generations for the city to open itself up to the outside world, figuratively and literally. The destruction of the wall will give way to new routes that will facilitate trade.

It was mainly two men, Louis Giraud (1805-1883) and Paul de Vivie (1853-1930) who emancipated Pernes. Many farms will thus see the light of day and develop exponentially, some even exporting their local produce. But the two world wars damaged and endangered the daily lives of ordinary Pernois and the region's economy.

Today, and since the second half of the 20th century, there are no less than 25 buildings classified as Historical Monuments. The Pernois, like their citizens, knew how to keep the memory of this beautiful commune of Luberon, by creating many museums with various themes (11). Allowing history lovers to discover all the richness of this place.

From all the excursions I have been able to make since the beginning of this adventure, I have realised that there is nothing more wonderful than to physically visit the sites. The Internet will never be able to compete with this authenticity. And because of my stories, I take this opportunity to honour all those people who contribute to the memory of our ancestors. Without being chauvinistic, in Provence, and more generally in France, we are lucky to have places, monuments, a history with a great "H" envied and jealous by a large number of countries around the world. This is certainly one of the reasons why our country is one of the most visited destinations in the world!

Cucuron...

Cucuron: No, that's not the name of a cucurbit! But it is a small village that has dominated the Grand Luberon valley for centuries. On a more serious note, his patronym is said to have a Celtic origin, "Cuc" meaning "nipple". Even if this association of three syllables catches a bit when you pronounce them, it remains a magnificent cocoon that embellishes the tranquillity and the charm of Provence.

Area : 32 km²   Population : 1807

Although the current village dates back to 1004, its genesis can be traced back to prehistory, according to the remains found. But it was not until the thirteenth century that Cucuron began to implant himself beyond his fortified belt. Demographically, it peaked in 1719, with three thousand inhabitants. But the next year, the plague killed more than one-third of the population. Then the rural-urban exodus and World War I only exacerbated the desertification phenomenon. It was not until the 1960s that a new clientele, seduced by the quality of life, the 300 days of sunshine and the unusual charm of this village, decided to invest in this beautiful commune of Luberon.

When I started wandering the streets, a phrase immediately came to mind: "Bobo-Chic." Sometimes it is true that it can have a pejorative connotation. But in this case, I have to say that the whole nobility of the term has taken over. Shop fronts are like shop owners, a perfect mix of "too much" and "not enough." Everything is refined, nothing is left to chance. In addition, they have managed to preserve the authenticity of the façades and monuments by adding a subtle touch of modernity, without however distorting the original aspect.

The icing on the cake that day was the empty attic around the Bassin de l'Etang. I don't know about you, but when I chase unusual objects, I often find myself wondering about their history, their experience, their origin. Who were their successive owners? Would I be next? And that's where the exhibitor comes in, aiming to tip the scales in the direction: "Okay, I'm buying it!"

As I walked through the streets of Cucuron, I quickly saw that I was facing a fireworks display of historic monuments, perfectly preserved, despite the time and events of the past. First of all, the 15th century Etang Basin, which I was talking about earlier. Although today it is a place where you can enjoy daydreaming alone or with friends, it used to be a water reserve used to feed the flour mill. But it is by entering the village that the village will reveal all its treasures to you.

First of all, the Donjon St Michel, abandoned in the 17th century by the family of Oraison, whose ruins were bought by a private individual in 1791, and then classified as a Historical Monument in 1921. Climbing up the heights of the village, you can visit the church of Notre Dame de Beaulieu. The building, whose parts have been added successively over the centuries, is unique in that it is a mixture of several styles. For history buffs, I invite you to discover the Musée Marc Deydier (1845-1920) which took up residence in 1970 in a 17th century mansion. You will find a collection of archaeological remains from the Neolithic and Bronze Age civilisation, as well as furniture dating back to the Roman period.

To conclude, I would say that Cucuron reminds me of a Russian doll. We go from discovery to discovery, from surprise to surprise. It's as if every monument, every stone, that helped build this village, made it your mission to make this visit forever etched in your mind.

Le Castellet...

Even if since the beginning of this adventure, I prefer places often unknown of our beautiful Provence, there remains one, despite its well-established notoriety, that I will encourage you to visit: Le Castellet. 'Lou Castellet' ('Petit Château' in Provençal) is a must-see on the Var coast.

It is difficult not to fall under the charm of this mediaeval city of the 12th century which dominates, from its height of 250 metres, the valley and the Mediterranean coastline. The municipality only owned the site in the 18th century. And it was not until 1939 that his inscription at the Monuments Historiques was approved.

Area : 44 km²   Population : 3920

Personally, when I go there, I prefer to park in the car park downstairs. This allows me to admire this magnificent washroom, centuries old. Whenever I see this beautiful building, I imagine women washing their belongings with their washing machines, taking advantage of this "meeting" to peddle the last gossip of the village. That's when you think that gossip didn't wait for the phone and social media to exist!

Le Castellet, located in the centre of the natural amphitheatre "Le Vignoble de Bandol" and the beginnings of the Sainte Baume, quickly turned to viticulture and olive growing. AOC wines and Provence AOC olive oil have been produced and exported around the world for several generations now.

In 1938, Marcel Pagnol chose this picturesque town to shoot "La Femme du boulanger" with Raimu and Ginette Leclerc.

In 1998, Patrice Leconte directed "One chance out of two" with Jean-Paul Belmondo, Alain Delon and Vanessa Paradis. And in 2011, Olivier Baroux will set up his cameras for "Les Tuche" with Jean-Paul Rouve and Isabelle Nanty.

Paul Ricard, an industrialist and inventor of this famous beverage, which was so popular among Marseille residents, had an automobile circuit built there in 1970 to host Formula 1 races.

Although the summer season remains favourable to a higher number of visitors, "Lou Castellet" remains a lively place from spring to autumn.

Almost all year round, you will have the pleasure of strolling through cobbled streets to admire these stone façades that have aged for centuries.

You will discover monuments that have known how to go through the ages, such as "Le Trou de Madame" (strange name, I grant you!) which is part of the multiple openings in the ramparts, its parish church of the Transfiguration dating back to the late 11th century, to which a nave was added in 1754. And if you are like me, a bit dreamer, surprise yourself to put in pictures everything these buildings could tell you if they could speak!

But Le Castellet is also a place where you can have lunch or dinner in peace. Indeed, restaurateurs have made every effort to choose the ideal place, such as a small square surrounded by the harmony of its façades, a terrace with trees facing an extraordinary panorama, for the sole purpose of making you taste their culinary creations.

For many decades, "Lou Castellet" has built a reputation based on the quality, originality and diversity of its craftsmanship. Moreover, its creators were able to highlight an architecture that seems to be frozen in the past, by setting up shops all more original than each other. Personally, it is always difficult for me to resist all these multi-ethnic creations such as jewellery, sculptures, paintings, etc. that come to land before my eyes.

You will have understood that this little jewel that Mother Nature and man have fashioned for several centuries will easily take you back in time, thanks to the monuments and façades that have passed through time so well.

La Ciotat...

I must admit that it was with a sweet mixture of tenderness and nostalgia that I realised this chapter. It was like walking in the footsteps of my childhood. Because my grandparents once lived in La Ciotat, I was lucky to spend almost all my school holidays there. Throughout the day, I played juxtaposing a child's experience with that of a young person in their fifties. On the Port-Vieux, I saw my grandfather waiting for Polo's trawler.

Area : 35 km²   Population : 35580

We never left without a Nylon bag full of sardines or mackerel, "offered by the house". My grandmother used to cook them in Escabèche sauce. I don't even count the number of times I went shopping with her on Rue des Poilus, a famous shopping street in the city centre. After shopping, we were going to join "grandpa" at the boulomane and we were all going back together by car. What wonderful memories!

Although today Ciotat has taken a 180° turn to become a seaside resort, this has not always been the case. Quite the contrary!

The city experienced a major population boom in the sixteenth century. Indeed, following local revolutions, the Genoese aristocracy was forced to leave Italy and settle in the Mediterranean city.

The first shipyards date back to 1622. They developed gradually until the beginning of the eighteenth century. Then comes a much more complicated period for citizens. But it is thanks to the transformation and modernisation of the site that they will become, until the 20th century, the main activity of Ciotat. However, the 1980s will be a crisis like no other. The economic and social repercussions will be irreversible, even tragic for some. The unions will do everything in their power to try to save their business by organising numerous demonstrations, some of which are particularly muscular. Attempts at negotiations will be made. Many families will be left behind, forced to sell their property in order to move and try to rebuild elsewhere. Some employees will even commit suicide.

But, as they say, the misfortune of some often makes the happiness of others. And the collapse of the real-estate sector will enable "benevolent" people to seep into families and build their fortunes.

However, despite these many setbacks, La Ciotat will manage to rise from the ashes, by directing its industry towards the manufacture of luxury boats. Once a working-class city, it has gradually transformed into a seaside resort. Many projects such as hotels, luxurious residences, a casino, the rehabilitation of the sheds of the former construction site into "trendy" restaurants/breweries, etc... have thus been able to see the light of day.

I told you about the bullfighter where my grandfather spent almost every afternoon. You should know that the "petanque" that would come "with feet trapped in the ground" to pull the ball, is a bit the "national sport" in La Ciotat. It is even said that it was born in June 1910 thanks to Jules Lenoir who, suffering from lower limbs, could not help but throw her with his feet still. I wouldn't be able to tell you if this legend is true, but I think it's a great story! What do you think?

If you stroll along the beach, you will probably come across a statue of Louis and Auguste Lumière, made in homage to these two brothers who invented the cinematographer. For the record, it was on September 21, 1895 that they projected in their Ciotaden property "The arrival of the train at the station of La Ciotat". I let you imagine the reaction of the few spectators present that day! Then, on December 28 of the same year, the first public session will be held at the "Grand Café" in Paris. This is the birth of the 7th art!

Every August 16, for nearly 300 years, the city organises jousting tournaments on the Old Port. This annual event is a very important event for the municipality, as it attracts a very large audience. For the record, the first official jousting club only dates back to September 1921.

La Ciotat is also the Ile Verte, opposite the Port Vieux, which is only accessible by boat. A particularly pleasant place where you can admire the sea floor, have a picnic on the sand, or have lunch in the only small restaurant. Just next to it, you can admire this huge rock in the shape of a bird's beak, hence "the Bec de l'Aigle". To see it more closely, I advise you to go to the Parc du Mugel. It remained private until 1987 and is now managed by the municipality. No less than 17 hectares protected and regulated welcome you every day (from 8 am to 8 pm) to swim in transparent water, or to go hiking in a sublime natural setting. And it was for its microclimate that residents came up with the idea of creating a free, landscaped botanical garden that now includes many varieties of exotic plants and trees.

When I think back to the history of La Ciotat, I think to myself that this city is like a Phoenix. Once a worker, it came very close to being the victim of an irreversible economic crisis, causing a dying population to swirl around and turn into a ghost town, like some mining communities in northern France. Today, it has become a seaside resort that is increasingly popular with foreigners. I invite you to take the time to discover it alone, as a couple or with your family. You will be able to build beautiful memories that you will tell, why not ... to your descendants.

Saignon...

To be honest with you, I have to admit that when I arrived in Saignon, I did not feel the usual "wow". But "I" is a personal emotion, so.... It's a bit like when you're faced with a work of art, you like it, you don't like it, or you're divided between two emotions. This is exactly what I experienced when I arrived in this Vauclusian village!

But what you can never take away from a site is its history, as well as its authenticity.

Area : 19 km²   Population : 1012

When you arrive in Saignon, you will see that what makes the place special is its location. Built around its rock nicknamed "Belle Vue", the village used to have as its main function to watch over the entire valley. In the past, the municipality was mainly used as an observatory. The first castrum (fortified place in Latin) was built on the rock in the Xth century. It will then be replaced by three forts, which is rare on such a small enclosure.

Nowadays, these remains are very popular with tourists. They offer a magnificent panorama of the whole plain.

The main square of the village, also called the "Grande Fontaine" square, has an architectural singularity. Indeed, if you look at the facades in detail, you will notice that one of them bears allegorical statues (depicting an abstract idea in concrete), in tribute to agriculture and industry. These artistic prowess were realised by a local artist, Elzéar Sollier. In addition, many of these exterior walls display vegetation that changes colour with the seasons. Depending on the time of year, these 'plant walls' change from green to yellow to red. A true visual feast for photographers and painters.

When I visit a village, I cannot tell you why, but I always look for a wash house. Perhaps that is because they used to be a meeting place, where people would take the time to chat while beating the laundry. And the one in Saignon has the particularity of being under a house. Today, it coexists with a "sharing library." The books are available to everyone. We take, we read and we rest! It's as if books had set themselves the mission of telling old stories.

On some streets, you may feel like time has stopped. But not necessarily in the noble sense of the word. I do not mean to be disparaging, but I think that the people who live there should renovate some of the buildings. Then they could recover their lustre from the past. But that's just me!

At the entrance to the village, you will discover the Romanesque church of Notre Dame. Built in the Middle Ages, it was an important stop for pilgrims from Rome to Santiago de Compostela. However, I would have liked to talk to you about its interior, but to my regret it was closed to the public: too bad! I guess it's because it has a reliquary of the Holy Cross. The church does not want to tempt the "Devil"!

Economically, agriculture is Saignon's strong point. Vines, cherry trees, cereals, lavender and truffle oaks have been cultivated here for many generations. High-quality honey and goat cheese, made on site, have long been the delight of gourmets. It should be noted that until the Second World War, a sulphur mine was exploited for the benefit of wine growers.

As you will have understood, Saignon is not part of the "top ten" sites that I have been able to visit since the beginning of this adventure. But I do not pretend to have the word of the gospel! That's why I invite you to discover this village in order to make your own opinion. Take the time to stroll through these streets with worn-out stones, often distorted by centuries of existence. If you come from far away, you can even book a stay in one of the many guest rooms in the town. I am convinced that history buffs, old façades and vestiges will succumb to Saignon's atypism.

Bormes-les-Mimosas...

I had heard about Bormes-les-Mimosas for a very long time, without ever having had the opportunity to visit it. For me, this commune can be summed up in one word: Sublime!

Area : 97 km²   Population : 8097

The first thing that struck me when I discovered Bormes was this panorama that combines refinement and sobriety. You will be amazed by its landscape where, in the greatest harmony, you will find huge villas, wine estates, farms and of course the famous Fort de Brégançon. All protected by an azure blue coastline, where the Mediterranean sun seems to be reflected in complete tranquillity.

Historically, the origins of this Var town, which today is one of the most beautiful villages in France, can be traced back to 400 years BC. Because of its geographical location, it was populated for a very long time by fishermen. The village and its ramparts were not built until the 12th century. Then, from the 13th century, five dynasties succeeded one another to rule the village. The Lavandou, an adjacent commune, was once attached to Bormes. Wanting to fly on its own, it did not achieve "independence" until 1913, after six long years of unsuccessful waiting. In the same year, Bormes and Hyères will be among the first French municipalities to be classified as 'Climate Station', due to their particularly mild winter climate.

For the record, "the Mimosas" will join Bormes in 1968. The residents probably wanted to pay tribute to this tree, derived from acacia, which is very present in the commune.

When you arrive in Bormes-les-Mimosas, you feel calm and serene. The inhabitants are smiling and welcoming. The façades are a sweet compromise between Italian and Provençal style, proudly displaying bright and warm colours. Shop owners are full of imagination to make their windows as attractive and unique as possible. When you pass by a restaurant, it is difficult to resist the Mediterranean scents that discreetly tickle your nostrils. If I can give you a piece of advice, don't "throw" yourself on the first deck that's available to you. Explore the colourful alleyways and discover real little nuggets of local gastronomy that will, I am sure, leave your taste buds numb.

But Bormes is not just a French Riviera town that looks like a movie set. It is also a place where you will discover artists, thanks to a painting workshop, a glass craftsman and small intimate galleries. Not to mention its weekly market (and nocturnal in summer) where products are presented that bear witness to our traditions, which purists have been striving to make endure for many generations.

For lovers of old stones, you can visit the Roman-style chapel of Saint Francis de Paule, built in 1560 in tribute to St. Francis for having liberated the city from the plague in 1481. Or at 324 metres, the chapel of Notre Dame de Constance, very popular among hikers because it offers a magnificent panorama, as well as a orienteering table. Although it is closed to the public, you will also have the opportunity to admire the Castle of the Lords of Fos, built between the 13th and the 14th centuries and classified as a historical monument since the beginning of the 30s.

Nature lovers and good wines will have the opportunity to stroll through the vineyards of the commune to admire the famous Côtes de Provence. And why not leave with some bottled souvenirs directly at the farmer's house.

However, there is one building that is difficult to separate from this Var site: the Fort de Brégançon (10)! Rented in the early 1920s by Senator Bellanger, it was entirely refurbished with his own money. However, he was forced by General De Gaulle to leave the house in the 1970s. Under the spell of the building and its 35-metre-high rocky peak, the Head of State will make it a holiday spot for the country's incumbent presidents. It will therefore order the construction of an artificial jetty to facilitate access to it, as well as a car park for staff (also serving as a heliport). The site can be visited on certain days of the week, at very specific times.

As I said earlier, I'm not a fan of places that have a large tourism population. But on that day, I had the privilege of living in a small town where Mediterranean roots are deeply rooted in minds, in architecture. A place where people still take the time to sit down and enjoy the life that is slowly flowing before their eyes, so they can enjoy it every moment. In short, a little piece of paradise that perspires bliss!

Le Beaucet...

However, you will have to drive about ten kilometres on a winding and narrow road to finally reach the foot of this small village on the hillside, full of charm and uniqueness. The first image that came to my mind was Mother Nature's, which set her sights on this place, so that man could build a life-size nursery.

Area : 9 km²   Population : 360

Don't expect to find a market town where souvenir shops and restaurants share every square metre, as in most tourist sites. I would say that Le Beaucet is more of a hiking spot. Kind of like a step where it would be possible to cut yourself off from the world for a few hours.

When I arrived, my eyes were immediately drawn to the castle. Perhaps that is because it produces a sense of patriarchal protection, like a wolf protecting a young child.

When I go to a site for the first time, I like to watch people above all. And then I realised that the time seemed to be almost slowing down. That tourists, like locals, took the time to appreciate every moment they were offered. Relaxing in peace this duality between past and present.

It is a real delight to be able to stroll through the alleys exhibiting façades that have aged over centuries of existence, where vegetation has gradually regained its sovereignty by covering the stones surreptitiously.

According to the traces found by archaeologists in the 20th century, the origin of the Beaucetans dates back to 8,000 years. But it was only in the Middle Ages that the village began to be built around its church and castle. A village community will then form near the building, seeking protection, as well as economic activity mainly focused on agriculture.

In the 16th century, Beaucet was heavily affected by religious wars. After many damage, the castle was regularly restored over the next two centuries. But in the eighteenth century, due to a lack of resources, its maintenance will cease to make way for vestiges that can be visited today. In all honesty, don't expect anything special! Only a few rooms housing mediaeval relics have been preserved.

It was not until the second half of the 19th century that the municipality experienced a new demographic boom. Indeed, growing wheat, vines, olive trees, and raising sheep and silkworms will enable villagers to expand their economic activity considerably for decades to come. But the two world wars will leave Beausetaine's population weak, because many men would go to the front lines and never return. In 1954, only 79 people lived in Beaucet. Then, in the early 1970's, major urban-planning projects, together with the development of tourism, helped to attract a new clientele. Young pensioners and the chic bobos of the time will appreciate the benefits of the countryside and nature. Today, there are no less than 360 inhabitants, all CSPs (occupational social categories) and ages combined, living in the village.

As I said earlier, for lunch, don't expect to have a choice between several restaurants/brasseries! Indeed, you have two options. You can either enjoy your picnic in front of a magnificent natural painting, or sit on the terrace of the only establishment. The owner will offer you a menu, also unique, composed of local products. Then you love it, or you don't! Personally, I am a fan of this type of atmosphere! The welcome is warm, and the products are of excellent quality. Tip, do not do as I do, plan a payment method other than the CB ...

As you will have gathered, when you go to the Beaucet, you will feel like you have done a good job in the past. You will rediscover the values of a time when we knew how to appreciate, in all humility, what presented itself to us. In short, a small corner of Paradise cut off from the world, offering the flora and fauna the opportunity to live in total harmony with man.

Saint-Rémy-de-Provence...

Saint-Rémy-de-Provence is said to be the capital of the Alpilles. In addition to being a concentrate of history, its Natural Park, classified since 2007, is home to a very wide variety of fauna and flora. If you stroll around this beautiful natural setting, you may be lucky enough to spot a felled lizard, a Egyptian vulture, a kestrel falcon, or even an owl. In 1992, no less than 800 plant species were listed by botanist Bernard Girerd in the Alpilles. Needless to say, all these species are protected, so: Don't touch! The bats, which are very present on the site, prefer to live together peacefully with the villagers.

Area : 89 km²   Population : 9612

The cave engravings and paintings from the Neolithic and Bronze Age found in Otello Cave suggest that Saint Remy's origins date back to prehistory.

In order not to make reading my text too tedious, I would refrain from recounting the period from the Middle Ages to royalty. It is both very informative and eventful, but it is more intended for history buffs! However, there is a date that remains inseparable from the municipality: December 14, 1503. It corresponds to the birth of the famous astrologer-doctor Michel de Nostredame, better known as Nostradamus. An Israelite by confession, he converted to Catholicism before being knighted. However, the famous apothecary lived, died and was buried in 1566 in Salon-de-Provence. The house of his childhood remains always visible in Saint-Rémy.

In 1720 and 1721, the city experienced its largest plague epidemic. Nearly a third of the population will be cured of the disease.

Economically, it was not until the nineteenth century that the city reached its "zenith," owing to the cultivation of black coal (a type of herbaceous plant) and its seeds. The numerous extensions carried out on the Alpilles Canal have largely benefited the sector. Due to the relationship between cause and effect, a large number of families of traders will come to settle and build large properties outside the ramparts. This will expand their trade with the rest of Europe and parts of the US. But World War I came to grip this affluence.

On a cultural level, St-Rémy has welcomed many artists throughout its history. But there is one that has left a profound impression on people: the Dutch painter Vincent Van Gogh. Interned in 1889 at the Saint-Paul-de-Mausole health home for mental disorders, he made several of his famous paintings during his stay. I highly recommend that you visit this building. As well as having the opportunity to see the painter's bedroom and bathroom, you will also discover an atypical building. And if, like me, you are sensitive to old stones, you will certainly feel something mystical when entering this cloister and walking through the corridors of this old hospice. It is as if the souls of its residents, who were once suffering, had left their mark on the building's DNA forever.

This Provençal "capital" has the particularity of satisfying the tastes of everyone. At the gates of St-Rémy lies the "Site de Glanum" . The updating of these archaeological remains will require more than a century of research. Thanks to this determination transmitted over several generations, the commune was able to dig up a Gallic city dating from the 2nd of our era with Greek and then Roman influences. Legend has it that there is a so-called miraculous source on Glanum. However, what is real is that this perfectly maintained place can be visited at a price that can be a budget for an entire family.

As you explore the area, you will find that in addition to the many souvenir shops, craft shops, artists' galleries and restaurants open to tourists, you will also have the opportunity to visit many monuments that span centuries in origin. This, in my opinion, accentuates their uniqueness. Of course, I won't be able to list them all!

Among them, however, is the Collegiate Church of Saint-Martin, which was rebuilt in 1821 in the Neo-Classical style of the time. Then if you want to improve your knowledge of Glanum, I would recommend you (only in season) to visit the Hotel de Sade. This 15th-century mansion houses archaeological pieces from the excavations of the site. Or the Regional Ethnological Museum of the Alpilles which will offer you a magnificent interior courtyard finely carved. And why not, the Jean de Renaud Chapel, of flamboyant Gothic style with its 14th century bell tower, which turned out to be the only vestige of the old church collapsed in 1818.

So if you want to discover, or rediscover, all these beautiful witnesses of the past. If you want to be welcomed by locals who love the heritage of this place above all. So I recommend that you book a short stay in one of the many guest rooms or hotels that this beautiful Provencal commune will make available to you.

Vaison-la-Romaine...

When you arrive at the gates of Vaison-la-Romaine, you should bear in mind that you are going to encounter 2,000 years of history. Three distinct parts, the ancient city, the mediaeval city and the modern city, have learned to live together in total harmony throughout these centuries, thus succeeding in creating a place highly appreciated by tourists and recognised beyond our borders.

Area : 27 km²   Population : 6046

It is said that Rome was not built in a day! Vaison-la-Romaine, too! Indeed, its origins date back to the fourth century BC. If I am referring to Rome, it is not by chance, because it is the Romans who will make the site one of the richest cities of Narbonnaise Gaul.

In 1645 will be founded in this same cathedral "the Brotherhood of Monsignor Vincent". Only "good Catholics and...believers" could be enthroned. With no less than 180 members when it was founded, its number declined steadily over the following decades, to 41 supporters in 1791.

It was not until the 18th century that the majority of the population returned to the plain. Two centuries later, it will take on the appearance of a true Vauclusian city, thus becoming a perfect compromise between past and present.

With an economy mainly orientated towards wine-growing and tourism, the "modern city" will see its expansion in the 1930s, thanks to its architectural style.

But a date will forever mark the minds and hearts of the people of Lyon. On September 22, 1992, an unprecedented deadly flood resulted in 37 deaths and four missing. The rising waters of the Ouèze River were as intense as they were rapid. Material losses will amount to €70 million. When you look at the façades overlooking the river, you can still see the stigmas left by Mother Nature. Some homes have not even been rebuilt, keeping in mind that everything can tip over in a matter of minutes.

To access the mediaeval city, you will have to cross the bridge which represents an entity. The building, listed as a historical monument since 1840, was built in the 1st century AD. During World War II, it came close to being fatally bombed by the German army. However, it was not until 1953 that the renovation work on the vault and the replacement of a few claves (cornered stones) were carried out.

That day, I had lunch at a restaurant-pizzeria at the foot of the ramparts. When I sat down, it was as if I was in the middle of a period film. As if I were going back in time in peace. And with some emotion, I must admit it! Because there is an atmosphere emerging from these colossal walls that I cannot explain.

But if you want to visit two millennia of history in peace, I advise you to spend a night on Vaison. There is no shortage of bed and breakfasts and hotels! You will take the time to discover the vestiges, museums, places of worship, art galleries … Not forgetting the souvenir shops of all kinds that will make your stay an unforgettable moment!

To name but a few, you will have the opportunity to visit the Gallo-Roman site of Puymin, the Theo-Desplans archaeological museum, the Notre-Dame-de-Nazareth Cathedral with its cloister, the Sainte-Marie-de-l'Assomption Cathedral, the Gallery of Limonadiers or Zanella Léon.

Vaison-la-Romaine, is a place where you have to take the time to appreciate every moment, so that this beautiful Lady of 2000 years can reveal all its mysteries and secrets. When you change the epoch from the ancient to the mediaeval and then modern, try to let go. Perhaps you will hear Vaison assure you in ear some beautiful legends that have gone through so many centuries!

Gordes et Village des Bories...

Gordes is a Vauclusian village in the heart of Luberon. The many artists who painted or photographed it have made it possible to immortalise it over the centuries, even to bring it back to life. I'll explain why...!

Even before reaching the village gates, you can admire several kilometres of "dry stone" walls (stones assembled without mortar), which stand between the road and magnificent properties.

Area : 48 km²   Population : 1873

At the centre of this worthy representative of the Provencal villages stands "Le Château". This imposing building from the Gallo-Roman era still seems to provide protection and prosperity to its villagers, like a lord of yesteryear. Historically, Gordes was tasked with protecting Cavaillon and accommodating its inhabitants during invasions.

It was in the 18th century that it reached its economic peak with olive cultivation, silkworm breeding and leather crafts. But in the nineteenth century, hard times began. The main cause of this decline will be rural-to-urban migration and the destruction caused by World War I. In addition, a succession of events will gradually put Gordes into oblivion. But in 1940, André Lhote, famous painter and writer, will have a crush on this beautiful Provençal town. In his emotional whirlwind, he trained a large number of intellectuals and artists from different worlds. Now, even though Gordes remains attached to its terroir and traditions, it has become a "chic place", in the noble sense of the term. And this contrast makes it an atypical and charming place. But this Vauclusian town wouldn't be what it is today if locals hadn't maintained local customs by organising year-round festivals, village festivals, cultural events, and even a Christmas Eve.

This is certainly one of the reasons why the site is now part of the very closed circle of the Most Beautiful Villages of France!

When I see a place full of history, I make sure to park outside. So I take the time to soak up the place slowly. If I were to compare Gordes to a geometric shape, I would think of it as a dome. Because it is thanks to the intertwined calades (steep streets paved with pebbles) that you will discover a unique village. As in an open-air maze, you will find yourself in a "cul de sac", sometimes "nose to nose" with a magnificent panorama of the Luberon valley.

A word of advice: choose very comfortable shoes!

After having lunch, I went to Sénanque Abbey. She is one of the three Cistercian "sisters" of Provence, along with Thoronet Abbey and Silvacane Abbey. Only a few kilometres of particularly winding and narrow roads separate the village of Sénanque. This 12th century building can be visited at certain times. You will also have the opportunity to discover its shop and its regional products, made largely on the abbey grounds. As a keen honey lover, I couldn't help but leave with 1 kg of this delicious nectar. After all, it is for the good cause, since the recipes of the shop and visits are used to maintain the monument!

Earlier, I was referring to these walls made of dry stone. Indeed, it is difficult to separate Gordes from its famous "Village des Bories", also called the "Black Village". Like a hamlet in the middle of scrubland and holm oaks, these thirty buildings were designed to house farmers during the agricultural season. Despite its Spartan side, each shed had a pre-established function. There were barns, barns, granaries, furnaces, vats, grinders, chicken coops and of course basic housing. Thus during the season, a real village life was born. But in the nineteenth century, its activities eventually collapsed and were finally abandoned.

It will take more than a century for the landowner to do everything in his power to restore this architectural feat. The work will take nearly 10 years. Listed as a historical monument since 1977, tourists can still visit the site to admire a collection of antiques, a garden of aromatic plants, completely renovated houses. That way, they could see how tough old life could be.

If you, like me, have the chance to visit Gordes, you will realise how important it is to respect André Lhote's memory. Because it is thanks to this artist that this forgotten village can today make the junction between the past, the present and I hope for the future...

Thanks...

It took me almost fifteen months to complete this "tour of the great dukes" that was so dear to my heart. Through this work, I have had the privilege of discovering wonderful and unusual places. Provençals fighting to preserve their traditions and their DNA. Places built on a history unlike any other. Okay, I'm a little chauvinistic on this one!

But I couldn't have written this tour guide without the goodwill of some people. So I want to thank Albane P. for putting me in touch with the right people, Stephanie and Lionel. Because she immediately believed in my project.

Thank you to Véronique for taking the time to read my texts again and correct what needed to be corrected.

Muriel P., Frédéric T., Sébastien M., Valérie B., Albane P. for having the patience to read my first chapters and to encourage me to persevere.

And of course, all my social media friends who have supported me since the beginning of the adventure.

Fifteen months is fast and long at the same time, especially when you have regime declines and when doubts take hold. But all your positive vibes have given me the strength to put an end to this beautiful slice of life!

Rafael. F.